Our Changing World

THE TIMELINE LIBRARY

THE HISTORY OF MONEY

BY BARBARA A. SOMERVILL

1861
The Confederacy prints its own money in New York.

▲ 45 B.C.
Romans issue a coin honoring *Juno Moneta*.

▶ 1999
Twelve European countries agree to a common currency.

| 500 B.C. | A.D. 0 | 500 | 1000 | 1500 | 2000 |

Content Adviser: Paul S. Willen, PhD, Senior Economist, Federal Reserve Bank of Boston, Boston, Massachusetts

THE CHILD'S WORLD® • CHANHASSEN, MINNESOTA

The Child's World

Published in the United States of America by The Child's World®
PO Box 326 • Chanhassen, MN 55317-0326 • 800-599-READ • www.childsworld.com

ACKNOWLEDGMENTS
The Child's World®: Mary Berendes, Publishing Director

Editorial Directions, Inc.: E. Russell Primm, Editorial Director; Katie Marsico, Managing Editor and Line Editor; Judith Shiffer, Assistant Editor; Rory Mabin and Caroline Wood, Editorial Assistants; Susan Hindman, Copy Editor; Jennifer Martin, Proofreader; Judith Frisbee, Peter Garnham, Olivia Nellums, Chris Simms, and Stephen Carl Wender, Fact Checkers; Tim Griffin/IndexServ, Indexer; Cian Loughlin O'Day, Photo Researcher; Linda S. Koutris, Photo Selector

The Design Lab: Kathleen Petelinsek, Design and Art Production; Julia Goozen, Art Production Assistant

PHOTOS
Cover/frontispiece: left—Araldo de Luca/Corbis; center—Bettmann/Corbis; right—Josh Westrich/zefa/Corbis.

Interior: 7—Visual Arts Library, London/Alamy Images; 9—Inmagine/Alamy Images; 11, 13, 14, 19, 21—The Granger Collection; 12—Alfred Ko/Corbis; 15—Ali Meyer/Corbis; 17—Archivo Iconografico, S.A./Corbis; 22, 24, 26—Bettmann/Corbis; 23—Lance Nelson/Corbis; 27—Frederic Pitchal/Corbis Sygma; 29—Reuters/Corbis.

REGISTRATION

LIBRARY OF CONGRESS CATALOGING-IN-PUBLICATION DATA
Somervill, Barbara A.
  The history of money / By Barbara Somervill.
      p. cm. — (Our changing world—the timeline library)
  Includes index.
  ISBN 1-59296-439-7 (library bound : alk. paper)
  1. Money—History—Juvenile literature. I. Title. II. Series.
  HG221.5.S66 2006
  332.4'9—dc22   2005024782

TABLE OF CONTENTS

WHAT IS MONEY?

"Just write a check," said LaShonda. She wanted new jeans.

"A check guarantees that you have the money to cover the cost in your bank. I don't have an extra $25 in my bank right now," said Mom.

"Then, you can charge it," said LaShonda.

"True," said Mom, "but charging just means I have to pay the money later. Credit is an agreement to pay tomorrow for what you buy today. But you still have to pay the money. If you want the jeans, earn the money to buy them."

LaShonda agreed to work for the money and save to buy the jeans. Mom set up a list of chores and the amount of money to be paid for each chore. Doing the dishes for a week paid $5. Cleaning the bathroom paid $3. Folding the laundry earned $2.

LaShonda began by cleaning the bathroom. "Okay, Mom," she said. "That will be $3." She put out her hand to get paid.

Mom took three large plastic paperclips out of her handbag and gave them to LaShonda. "Mom, this isn't money!" LaShonda complained.

Mom smiled. "No, it's plastic—just like a credit card is plastic. For this contract, I'm paying you in paperclips. Each clip is worth $1. When you have $25 worth of clips, we'll go buy the jeans. The clips are like money, only you can't spend them outside our house."

LaShonda wasn't happy. She wanted real money—dollar bills or a handful of coins. Mom pointed out that many things have been considered money in different cultures: shells, large stones, gold dust, and even salt.

"Money is just items that represent certain values. You can use those items to buy goods or services. If we say the paperclips are worth a dollar each, they are like money. They represent your ability to buy the jeans—just like cowrie shells or an ounce of gold dust," explained Mom. "You need $25 to buy the jeans—or, in this case, 25 paperclips."

"But, suppose I change my mind and want to spend what I earn on something else?" LaShonda asked.

"Well, you can't spend paperclips at a store. The bank of Mom will just have to exchange that plastic for paper—paper money that is," said Mom.

CHAPTER ONE

SEASHELLS AND GOLD INGOTS

Ten thousand years ago, people had no need for money. They were hunter-gatherers. This meant that they hunted meat, fished, and collected fruits, nuts, and berries. They lived in caves or simple huts and moved as the seasons changed.

Even when people settled into villages, they still had no need for money. Villagers grew, made, and built everything they could. Whatever they could not produce themselves, they traded, or **bartered,** for. Lurg traded three dried codfish for a wheel of cheese. Olla bartered cloth with Mitt, who then fixed the hole in her roof.

As villages expanded into cities, the need for trade only increased. One person made shoes, another grew vegetables, and another ground grain into

ca. 8000 B.C.	ca. 4000 B.C.

People are hunter-gatherers.

Grain farming begins in present-day Israel.

People barter for goods and services.

The wheel is developed in the Middle East.

flour. As people had more items to trade, bartering became more complicated.

2500 B.C.: IN PLACE OF MONEY

Money still did not exist in the form of coins and bills. People continued to trade items instead of exchanging money. Peru's Incas paid with cloth. Ancient Norwegians paid with butter, dried cod, or live animals. In parts of India, a handful of almonds bought a live chicken. Large, round stones were the preference of Yap Islanders—the bigger the stone, the greater its value. On the island of Naura, people used rats as money.

Cattle provided purchasing power in many cultures. A good cow paid taxes or bought a

Ancient accounting tables (right) reveal that Mesopotamians begin using a system of shekels, minas, and talents to set standard weights for gold and silver.

2500 B.C.

Central Americans begin farming corn.

7

bride. One or two fast horses bought a farm. Sheep, lla-
mas, yaks, and goats were also used as money. But paying
by goat was not always convenient.

Over time, gold and silver became especially popu-
lar for trade. By 2500 B.C., the Mesopotamians established
standard weights for gold and silver **ingots.** These were
metal clumps, ribbons, and shavings. Mesopotamian units
of weight were called *minas, shekels,* and *talents,* each with
standard values. Merchants could buy entire harvests of
grain with a handful of gold shekels.

About 2,300 years ago, the Egyptians also used standard gold and silver weights. Traveling merchants carried
small scales to measure gold, silver, or copper payments.

1500 B.C.

The Chinese use the cowrie
shell as a unit of money.

Egyptians use sundials to
tell time.

600 B.C.: CHINESE INGOTS

Like the Mesopotamians, the Chinese developed measures for precious metals. Gold and silver ingots in Asia took the shape of shells, flowers, lions, snails, and bullets.

But there were problems with ingots. Some people passed off cheap **base metals** as gold or silver. So merchants became hesitant to accept ingots. To assure merchants that ingots were pure, officials pressed seals into the metal.

The Chinese set standard weights for gold (right) and silver.

600 B.C.

The Greeks build a temple at Olympia.

Egyptians set standard weights for gold, silver, and copper.

ca. 300 B.C.

Greek geographer Pytheas concludes that ocean tides are controlled by the Moon.

CHAPTER TWO
COINS AND CASH

Sometime around 600 B.C., the Lydians of present-day Turkey had a great idea. Instead of distributing blobs of gold with seals, why not just make coins? The Lydians decided to make several standard sizes, each with a specific value.

Between 560 and 546 B.C., King Croesus of Lydia began **minting** separate gold and silver coins. These coins showed a lion's head and a bull's head facing each other.

Soon, the Greeks decided they would make coins, too. Athens' coins featured the symbol of the goddess Athena—the owl. Other cities pressed shapes of eagles, doves, bees, goats, and winged horses into coins.

| ca. 600 B.C. | 560–546 B.C. |

Lydians begin using coins.

The Hanging Gardens of Babylon are built.

King Croesus distributes separate gold and silver coins.

Plays are performed in Greece for the first time.

359–336 B.C.: PHILIP OF MACEDONIA

King Philip of Macedonia used coins to remind people in his empire who was in charge. He accomplished this by ordering his name printed on coins. The **obverse** featured a picture of the god Zeus that looked amazingly like Philip. The **reverse** showed Philip winning an Olympic chariot race.

Philip stopped short of adding his official profile to money. The first person to do that was Ptolemy I of Egypt in 306 B.C. A profile is a side-view of someone's head. After Ptolemy I, many world leaders ordered their profiles placed on coins. Money also sometimes featured leaders'

Philip of Macedonia orders his name printed on money.

359–336 B.C.

The Persians take over Egypt.

Ptolemy I (above) orders his profile printed on Egyptian money.

306 B.C.

Antigonus I declares himself king of Macedonia.

slogans, which were sayings that expressed their political views or beliefs.

CA. 200 B.C.: CHINESE SHOVELS AND HOES

In ancient China, people traded common bronze tools such as knives, shovels, and hoes. In about 200 B.C., the Chinese began minting coins in the shapes of tools. This was logical because selling tools brought wealth to China. Later, the Chinese added holes to their coins. People could string their money together, which made carrying it easier.

By 100 B.C., China suffered a shortage of base metal money, called cash. At that time, the term *cash* described Chinese coins. Today, it is often used to refer to dollar bills, or to talk about money in

12

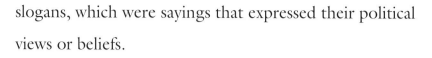

ca. 200 B.C.

The Chinese begin minting coins in the shape of tools (left).

The Second Macedonian War begins.

a general way. To offset the lack of cash, the Chinese tried something unique—leather money. They issued 1-square-foot (.9-square-meter) deerskins worth 40,000 coins. This was not successful. People wanted cash, not deerskin.

45 B.C.: THE ORIGINS OF THE WORD *MONEY*

In the last two centuries B.C., the Roman Empire spread throughout Europe. The Romans conquered other cultures. Some conquered people hated the Romans and responded by attacking them.

On one occasion, Roman soldiers were in a temple dedicated to the goddess Juno as enemy forces approached. As their enemy sneaked toward them, geese on the temple grounds took flight. The flutter

Romans issue a coin honoring *Juno Moneta* (right).

45 B.C.

Julius Caesar develops the Julian calendar; the year has 445 days.

of wings alerted the soldiers and saved them. Rome issued a coin honoring the event: *Juno Moneta,* or "Juno the Warner." Some historians believe that *Moneta* eventually developed into today's English word *money.*

Shortly after the occurrence in the temple, Roman leader Julius Caesar declared himself a god and wanted everyone to know it. In 44 B.C., he added the saying *Dict Perpetvo,* or "Dictator Forever," to Roman coins. A dictator is a ruler who has complete control over a nation. The coins had barely been released when Caesar was stabbed to death. One of his killers then issued coins that showed crossed daggers on the back. The daggers warned people not to call themselves gods.

30 B.C.

Roman poet Virgil (left) begins writing the *Aenid,* an epic of the founding of Rome.

CHAPTER THREE

PAPER MONEY

In A.D. 812, China suffered another coin shortage. China used coins to pay for goods coming into the country, which meant that cash left the country. To make up for the loss, China printed paper money. In 200 years, China issued paper money equal to nearly 3 million ounces (85 million grams) of silver.

But people didn't want paper money. They wanted cash. To make paper money more appealing, the Chinese mixed silk with paper to produce money that had a softer feel. They even added perfume.

By the late 1200s, Chinese citizens

China issues paper money in place of cash.

A.D. 812

Charlemagne (right) is emperor of the Holy Roman Empire in Europe.

15

> "In this city of Kanbalu is the mint of the grand [Kublai] Khan. . . . The coinage [printing] of this paper money is authenticated with as much form and ceremony as if it were actually pure gold or silver."
>
> —Marco Polo, explorer

accepted paper money. A paper bill worth 1,000 coins measured 9 inches by 13 inches (23 centimeters by 33 cm) and weighed barely 1 ounce (28 g). Chinese coins equal to that sum would have weighed 8 pounds (3.5 kilograms). It was therefore much easier to carry paper money than coins.

1605: BANK OF THE HOLY SPIRIT

By the mid-1300s, Europe was familiar with paper money. Most banks did not print paper **currency,** but religious groups, merchants, and traders did. English goldsmiths paid with their own paper money because it was safer than using gold. Gold could be taken and spent anywhere. The goldsmiths' paper money could be cashed only at one of the goldsmith's offices. In Japan, Buddhist and Shinto

| **1300s** | British goldsmiths issue paper money.

According to popular legend, Robin Hood roams England's Sherwood Forest. | **1304** | Marco Polo visits a Chinese mint at Kanbalu.

Using eyeglasses becomes a common practice. |

temples developed paper money. Even the pope got into the money business. In 1605, Pope Paul V began the Bank of the Holy Spirit. Since the Vatican is considered an independent country, this bank became the first national bank.

Traders during the 1600s were often responsible for making large payments. But no one wanted to ship chests of gold or silver over long distances. They could easily get lost or stolen. Instead, some businessmen handwrote personal paper money. This money was similar to today's checks. The signer guaranteed that the money was in a bank. The receiver gained access to the money by presenting the handwritten bill at the bank.

"MONEY NEVER MADE A MAN HAPPY YET, NOR WILL IT. THERE IS NOTHING IN ITS NATURE TO PRODUCE HAPPINESS. THE MORE A MAN HAS, THE MORE HE WANTS. INSTEAD OF FILLING A VACUUM, IT MAKES ONE."
—BENJAMIN FRANKLIN, INVENTOR AND U.S. POLITICIAN

1605

Pope Paul V establishes the Bank of the Holy Spirit.

Spain's Miguel de Cervantes publishes *Don Quixote* (right).

1690: COLONIAL MONEY

As the North American colonies grew, Great Britain developed a cash shortage. The British government didn't want coins leaving the country. But it did want its colonies to use British money. British currency was so scarce in the colonies that, in 1635, bullets called musket balls were accepted as **farthings.**

Instead of using cash, colonists bartered in grain, butter, cheese, tobacco, and wool. But colonial governments needed the cash. They could not pay for new roads, buildings, or docks with wheels of cheese.

In 1690, the Massachusetts Bay Colony started printing its own money. This upset Great Britain, so the

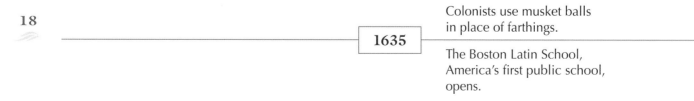

1635

Colonists use musket balls in place of farthings.

The Boston Latin School, America's first public school, opens.

Bay Colony promised not to print any more. But within a year, colonists there were back to producing paper money. Every colony joined the paper money business.

In 1703, South Carolina printed paper money to fund an attack against the Spanish at Saint Augustine, Florida. Whenever a colony needed to fund a project, it simply printed more money. Eventually, the money became worthless because there was no precious metal to back it up. The paper money turned into "bills of credit."

The Massachusetts Bay Colony commissions the first American coin, the Pine Tree Shilling (right), for use in local trade.

1652

Tea is introduced in Britain for the first time.

The Massachusetts Bay Colony prints its own paper money.

1690

French forces burn Schenectady, New York, during King William's War.

CHAPTER FOUR

GREENBACKS AND MOOLAH

Most countries have a monetary system. The government has expenses, and citizens need currency to buy goods and services. When the United States declared independence from Great Britain, it also needed its own currency. The first continental currency was issued in 1775. It was used to pay soldiers and to buy weapons and supplies for the Revolutionary War (1775–1783).

Once the war ended, Congress discussed establishing a permanent monetary system. In 1785, the U.S. government chose dollars and cents as the main currency. Congress established a mint to make U.S. money. Copper coins, minted in 1787, had a value of one cent. Some featured the motto "Mind Your Business." Silver dollars followed in 1794. In 1795, a $10 coin called the eagle

1775		1785	
The Continental Congress issues its own currency.		The United States establishes a monetary system based on dollars and cents.	
The first Revolutionary War battles occur at Lexington and Concord in Massachusetts.		New York City becomes the temporary capital of the United States.	

was introduced. Until 1913, though, banks still issued most paper money.

During the 1800s, the United States used several different currencies. Most people accepted gold and silver coins as "real" money. Banks issued paper money but promised to exchange paper for coins if asked. Unfortunately, many banks printed more paper money than they had coins available. This left no backup if a bank failed. For example, if the bank of Elm City ran out of money and closed, bank customers lost all their money. This was a serious problem.

The Civil War (1861–1865) divided

U.S. copper coins (right) are worth one cent.

1787

Architect James Hoban designs the White House.

the United States into North and South. Southern states broke away from the U.S. government and began their own government—the Confederacy. "Yankee" money referred to U.S. currency, which was used by Northerners (who were often called Yankees). The Southern states printed their own Confederate money.

The first Confederate notes included bills up to $1,000. The notes were printed by the National Bank Note Company—in the Yankee city of New York. When the war ended, Confederate money became worthless. No one wanted money from a government that no longer existed.

1852	The U.S. government issues $50 gold coins.	1861	The Confederacy prints its own money (left) in New York.
	Franklin Pierce wins the U.S. presidential election.		The Civil War begins in the United States.

1913: THE FEDERAL RESERVE SYSTEM

By 1913, the United States needed a federal bank system to control banking and money throughout the country. The Federal Reserve Act established a central bank and twelve district banks. It also set up gold deposits to back up the U.S. currency.

In 1938, the Federal Reserve made Fort Knox, Kentucky, the main gold storage center. Gold bars are kept in a bombproof, cement storage area called a bunker. Other secure storage areas called vaults house U.S. gold, but none have as much as Fort Knox.

DID YOU KNOW? EVERY WORKDAY, THE U.S. MINT MAKES 25 MILLION PENNIES, 2 MILLION NICKELS, 10 MILLION DIMES, AND 4 MILLION QUARTERS.

1913

Congress sets up the Federal Reserve (right).

Construction is completed on the Panama Canal.

U.S. currency has changed over the years. In the 1950s, "In God We Trust" was printed on U.S. money. The late 1970s saw the Susan B. Anthony dollar—a coin no one willingly used. The coin was too close to the same size as quarters, and people did not want to give up their paper dollars. In 2003, the design and ink colors on paper money changed. The U.S. Mint introduced a peach and blue version of the $20 bill. The new design is hard to copy, which should reduce **counterfeiting.**

Fort Knox (above) becomes the main vault used to store U.S. gold.

1938

Georg and Ladislao Biro invent the ballpoint pen.

CHAPTER FIVE

MONEY TODAY

The move toward "moneyless money" began in 1950 with a piece of plastic about 2 inches by 3 inches (5 cm by 7.5 cm). The plastic was a Diner's Club card—the first credit card. People who use credit cards to purchase things at stores and restaurants are later sent a bill for any items they bought. In 1950, the Diner's Club card could be used only at restaurants. By 1958, the credit card took hold. American Express came first and, in 1959, Bank of America's Visa joined the plastic money gang.

Not long after this, credit cards overwhelmed the economy. Soon people were paying for everything with plastic. It was safer than carrying large amounts of cash. People stopped living on today's money and enjoyed spending tomorrow's paycheck instead.

1950	1958
Diner's Club issues the first credit card.	American Express and Visa join the credit card business.
Charles Schultz draws the first *Peanuts* comic strip.	NASA is formed.

1968: REAL ATMs

Some people still preferred cash, but this wasn't always convenient because banks weren't open enough hours. Inventor Don Wetzel developed a successful automatic teller machine (ATM) in 1968. These machines allow bank customers to withdraw money or check their **balances** without having a bank employee help them. Some ATMs even let customers put money in their bank accounts! People liked the idea that banking could be done twenty-four hours a day, seven days a week.

More people also began carrying debit cards. A debit card works like a credit card but removes the amount of money spent directly from a bank account. Debit cards

FIRST NATIONAL CITY BANK

CITIBANK
introduces
'the Cash Station'

1968

Don Wetzel invents a
successful ATM (left).

Martin Luther King Jr.
is assassinated.

can be used at ATMs. Cardholders can charge gasoline, food, or clothing with a debit card. They just need to have enough money in their bank accounts.

Although many people felt safe carrying plastic money, credit card theft became a problem. In 1984, France introduced smart cards. These cards have magnetic strips along the back, coded with a personal identification number (PIN). They require users to punch in an identifying code. The next step in safer cards would be fingerprints or personal photographs.

1999: THE EURO

Twelve countries decided to give up their national currency in 1999 and replace it with a standard

France introduces the smart card (right).

1984

Kathryn Sullivan becomes the first woman astronaut from the United States to walk in space.

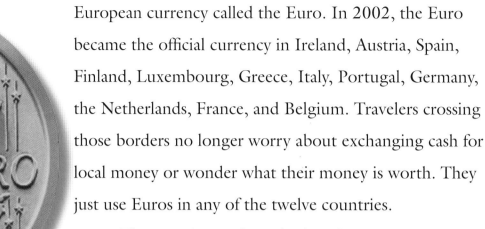

European currency called the Euro. In 2002, the Euro became the official currency in Ireland, Austria, Spain, Finland, Luxembourg, Greece, Italy, Portugal, Germany, the Netherlands, France, and Belgium. Travelers crossing those borders no longer worry about exchanging cash for local money or wonder what their money is worth. They just use Euros in any of the twelve countries.

The Euro is not the only shared currency. In recent years, Ecuador had serious financial problems. They decided to get rid of their own currency. Today, the U.S. dollar is Ecuador's official currency. Panama also uses U.S. dollars.

Around the world, dollars, yen,

1999

Twelve European countries agree to a common currency (left).

Holes by Louis Sachar wins the Newbery Medal.

pounds, rubles, and drachma are just a few of the currencies that fly from bank to business to government using computers. Computer money is transferred without cash ever physically moving from place to place.

For years, businesses paid their taxes over the Internet. Now anyone can. Many people's paychecks are automatically placed in their bank accounts. People pay bills over the Internet. They buy groceries, gas, clothing, pizza, and movies using plastic money. Someday, pennies, nickels, and dimes may no longer exist—all money will be "virtual" money. That will be quite a change from "Will you take two baskets of corn for that salmon?"

2000 — Ecuador chooses the U.S. dollar as its official currency.

Vladimir Putin (right) is elected president of Russia.

GLOSSARY

balances (BAL-uhnss-ez)
Balances are the amounts of money that people have in their bank accounts. People can use ATMs to check their bank balances.

bartered (BAR-terrd)
Someone who has bartered has traded for goods or services. A woman bartered cloth with a man who then fixed the hole in her roof.

base metals (BAYSS MET-uhlz)
Base metals are common metals of lesser value, such as lead or iron. The Chinese issued base metal coins, called cash.

counterfeiting (KOUN-tur-fit-ing)
Someone who is counterfeiting money is producing fake currency. Criminals have often counterfeited U.S. $20 bills.

currency (KUR-uhn-see)
Currency is the coins and bills that make up a nation's money. British currency includes pounds and pence.

farthings (FAR-thingz)
Farthings were coins that were worth one-fourth a British pence, or penny. Colonists used musket balls as farthings in 1635.

ingots (ING-uhtz)
Ingots are pieces of precious metal that were used as money. The Chinese used ingots that were shaped like snails and flowers.

minting (MINT-ing)
Minting is the process of making coins or printing paper money. Between 560 and 546 B.C., King Croesus of Lydia began minting coins.

obverse (ob-VURSS)
The obverse of a coin is also called the heads. The head of Zeus appeared on the obverse of Macedonian coins.

reverse (ri-VURSS)
The reverse of a coin is also called the tails. The reverse of a quarter features an eagle.

FOR FURTHER INFORMATION

AT THE LIBRARY

Nonfiction

* Allen, Larry. *Encyclopedia of Money*. Santa Barbara: ABC-CLIO, 1999.

Cribb, Joe. *Money*. New York: Knopf, 1990.

Giesecke, Ernestine. *From Seashells to Smart Cards: Money and Currency*. Chicago: Heinemann Library, 2003.

Godfrey, Neale S. *Neale S. Godfrey's Ultimate Kids' Money Book*. New York: Simon & Schuster Books for Young Readers, 1998.

* Weatherford, J. McIver. *The History of Money: From Sandstone to Cyberspace*. New York: Crown Publishers, 1997.

Fiction

Manes, Stephen. *Make Four Million Dollars by Next Thursday!* New York: Bantam Books, 1991.

* Books marked with a star are challenge reading material for those reading above grade level.

ON THE WEB

Visit our home page for lots of links about money: *http://www.childsworld.com/links*

Note to Parents, Teachers, and Librarians:
We routinely check our Web links to make sure they're safe, active sites—so encourage your readers to check them out!

PLACES TO VISIT OR CONTACT

Federal Reserve Bank of Richmond
701 East Byrd Street
Richmond, VA 23219
804/697-8000

National Numismatic (Coin) Collection
Smithsonian Institute
14th Street and Constitution Avenue NW
Washington, DC 20560
202/633-1000

The U.S. Mint
151 N. Independence Mall East
Philadelphia, PA 19106
215/408-0114

INDEX

ABOUT THE AUTHOR

BARBARA SOMERVILL IS THE AUTHOR OF MANY BOOKS FOR CHILDREN. SHE LOVES LEARNING AND SEES EVERY WRITING PROJECT AS A CHANCE TO LEARN NEW INFORMATION OR GAIN A NEW UNDERSTANDING. MS. SOMERVILL GREW UP IN NEW YORK STATE, BUT HAS ALSO LIVED IN TORONTO, CANADA; CANBERRA, AUSTRALIA; CALIFORNIA; AND SOUTH CAROLINA. SHE CURRENTLY LIVES WITH HER HUSBAND IN SIMPSONVILLE, SOUTH CAROLINA.